Gorgeous Nonsense

Table Of Contents

Dedicated to all who believed in me
All who championed me
All who gave me a second
I did my best to handle
Each one as if it
Were priceless
Which they
Are

I'm Gonna Make "It"

By the skin of my teeth
The sweat of my sack
The corrosion of my toe nails

Off the strength of a plastic bag
Through the valley painted on the brick wall
The grinded gears convinced they
Don't need lube

I'm gonna make "it"
I don't know what "it" is
What "it" is made of
Where "it" is

But I know I'm gonna make
It
A beacon to behold

The Conspiracy Theorists Were Right

Our leaders really ARE a masochist
Magic regime steamrolling protests of
Peace feeding blood to the owl
Putting its pellets in our groceries

We literally can't afford shit
Doomed from the start
Mud pies and fire flies from
A trashcan sparked
We have to kill each other just
To earn a voucher with more wrinkles than
A white flag used as a tissue

They treat us like ones and zeroes
They haven't played with our kids
Worked our jobs
They've only cut corners by
Cutting us off

They dance in ballrooms while we
Dance on hot coals
And when they get caught lying
They blow it off like latte foam

The truth sounds wicked these days
That's all I'm trying to say
But the conspiracy theorists clocked
It just the other day

Everything poisons you
All because greed mesmerizes the
Privileged and stiff arms the helpless

The truth sounds wicked I bet
That's by design
If they make the truth nonsensical
It'll amplify the lies
Hook line and
Sinker. God bless conspiracy theorists

Nothing At All

Death does not always
Scare the suicidal
Man
Occasionally it intrigues and
When the blue moon blossoms
It excites
Many are too afraid of the process of
Passing away   But the aftermath
The permanent serenity of
Nothing at all
In any way shape or form
Is truly thrilling
Some misinterpret the caution
We reserve towards the messy snuffing of
Our borrowed breaths
For the pining of the cushiony paradise
Which we are promised we have a
Reservation for

Death does not always
Scare the suicidal
Man
Sometimes it is the one thing keeping us
Alive

Equality Is Not Revenge

Equality is not revenge
Equality is not revenge
Equality is not revenge
Equality is not revenge
Equality is not revenge

But revenge is so gratifying
...
Isn't it?

The Lone Spark And The Lone Spark

I was once walking down the streets of
Soho New York with someone who used to
Be a friend
   And is now a memory I'm on good terms
   With

We came across a man bleeding
Profusely from his mushy abdomen
Writhing in eternal pain everybody stood
Around him. Not helping. But recording
Him with their phones. I asked
"Why ain't anyone helping him?"
They told me he didn't have the money
To afford the ambulance

I had a cigarette my last cigarette and the
Bleeding man saw it he begged me
"PLEASE PLEASE BEFORE THE REAPER
RIPS ME A NEW ONE CAN I GET
A CIGARETTE"
I told him I didn't have one and this
Seemed to make the blood flood faster

With nothing else to do I smoked my last
Cigarette as he died on the grimy lumpy
Calloused concrete
And I saw his spirit rise above to a
Hopefully more forgiving place I ashed
My cigarette and the remaining ember fell
To the ground at the same speed
Two lone sparks going back to where they
Came from

I decided to stop smoking cigarettes
That night

What Keeps Me Going

Nothing
I just go

I don't always have time to
Dedicate my tenacity to something
New
I know if I keep moving I'll intercept
A new reason sooner or later

And if the latter increases more
And   more
If I never find a reason to keep
Going maybe that's a weight off my
Shoulders I didn't know
                Was dragging me down
If it turns out I never had a reason
I'd be happier
                Better for it

Because what keeps me going
Is my WANT to go
I don't want anything to move me
I want to move

Cinematic Sadness

What's so entertaining about turmoil
    Anyways?
Is it the romanticization of relating to
Every sad song on your phone?

Elderly skies sapped of dimension crying
On your window pane
                Giving you the perfect backdrop
    To pose inspiringly   And power
Through a fresh tribulation

Sulking around in a black and white film
 Feeling the blues
            Trying to unscramble this depression
Into a lesson filled with the wisdom
                Of 1000 monks

Or do you romanticize your sadness
To feel like it all means something?
Could you bare the naked truth that it might
            Just be the wrong day?

Wish Like A Genie

I come from clouds like a genie
How I blame the ceramic
For all the stress I'm relieving
Recently the guillotine has me wishing
For sleep/It seems to me the bees
Slap their knees when they see me
Make mistakes and burden pain
From regret I've been gleaning/
I really wish the seasons change
Would bring benefits as
I've been pleading
But a wish upon a wish
Doesn't add up for the fiending/
I do my best to enact
Change, the future is leaning
Over my shoulder breathing
In my ear through their teeth
Not seeing, more like anticipating
Married sensibilities/
But I keep wishing
For it to change on its own
Like a wish from a genie

The Kids Are Not Okay

The kids are off whippets
And
Vyvanse
That's
How
BORED they are.
That's
How
MUCH they care.

The kids are not okay.
But they are creative.

Boring Depression

There's so many things I COULD
Be doing
There's so many things I SHOULD
Be doing
But I'm not sure what to start with

Hopefully some healthy habits
Kamikaze my frontal lobe
And the shockwave cracks the code

I'm out of orbit
Suspended in the echo chamber
Plastered with hallmark wallpaper
Unsupervised depression is not
Bittersweet glory
It is

Boring and sluggish

Divided House

Uneven pieces breaking up brawling
Pits like a machete cutting off
The weak wrist that
Never wanted
To feed
Us

But we're too baffled to paddle
Backwards
So we sort of remain stagnant
And wait for a few reactions
To turn our statistics into fractions

Divided

By audience claps
Compared to what is said
On stage...
Muffles pity with love and rubs friction
Against the skull until combustion
And shows a report with a failing
Grade.
Signed for approval with loose DNA
We could just get them next time
But a
House

Divided

Against itself can't win
I don't think that guy
Was as crazy as his top hat!

I fear and loathe
They might've known
That a house divided against itself
Is merely a house of fools.

The Ghost Of Bad News

This is a poem that you read when
It's pouring out
And it's the type that you recite
In the slaughterhouse

An apparition volunteered to be my
Sleep paralysis demon it's
                    The Ghost Of Bad News
Telling me that it doesn't get better
An explosion has happened in the
West coast
    Telling me unemployment's up
        Some children drowned
            Inflation has tripled
Telling me that it doesn't get better
                    The Ghost Of Bad News
            He damn sure is
But if I don't let him bother me I still
            Sleep still

His tricks don't work on me I'm
    Desensitized to his games
You can't teach an old dog new tricks
And
                    The Ghost Of Bad News
    Can't tell a happy story to save
            Either of our lives

Untitled

As the veil atrophies I go out on a
Limb.
As my creativity wanes my musings
Limn.
If the preeminent "block" squares it's
Shoulders.
I'll recite an affable rehearsal
If an empty page threatens me
I'll mold it into a mural
And if the format & delivery don't mesh
I'd never mind a burial.
When I stop writing I
Or creativity dies.
So I'll go out on a limb
And use it as an extra pen
When I write

Moth Ruler

Tyranny flopping lopsided
Acts as a doorstop
I can't
Get away.
I've been in the frail shriveling nest
So   Long
There
Is my new kitchen
Is my new community
Is my old friend
This pasty
Moth Ruler: The Great (In weight)
Soon to be overruled
Once I find a
Flamethrower in my|Humble abode

To All The Special People

I wish I was special
Out of this crowd of 8 billion
Killing themselves to make a killing
And still feel lonely
I'm just a civilian
I wish I was special like you, pray tell
How'd you do it? Get
Ordained out the womb
To be part of something bigger than
Yourself? And influence
Him, Her, They, It
Pairs, Crowds, Countries, Continents?
I know it wasn't common sense
No normal thinker ever stood out
Like tweakers on the corner catching
Second hand vape clouds
I wish I was special
But not SO fucking special
That I attract all the creeps
Who save a slot on their mantle for me
To live forever in taxidermy

I pickpocket in mosh pits
And get jealous when biopics
And documentaries make me compare
Myself to celebrities
I try to stay as grounded as I can
But there's no glow under sand
My arrogance needs its spotlight
And meaningful attention to mend
This desire of wanting
Wishing I was special when

I already am

Stimulating Reminders

When I selfishly allow a hibernation
Session to run longer than a paragraph
With no punctuation
I start to get restless and derealized
And start taking oxygen and vitamin D
For granted
To correct this feeling I know I must
Go get my heart broken
Pet another person's Pomeranian
Wade in the frothy ocean with my friends
Liberate my work week by getting drunk
On a Thursday
Chew bubblegum after getting a cavity
Filled
Get kicked in the sternum
Try a new food
Longboard over acorns, peelings in the
Pavement and dead larvae without falling
Off
Stand under a traffic helicopter and
Feel the chopping cyclical blades rattle
The parked cars and lost pets beneath it
I need some form of stimulation
I need to break the simulation
By proving there is no such thing
By proving that if I'm unhappy I don't
Have to project that hollow glitchy feeling
Onto what's around me
But remind myself I have a right to
Live my life   And   Heal myself

Here's To You, Perfect Pixie

I'll be rooting for you
But I won't be in the stands
I'll
Be bow-legged boastful
A little bitter and hyper
I'll be cheering at the screen
When you hoist that trophy
But if I get an invite to the after party
I'll let you know right now
It got lost in the mail

Here's to you
Perfect Pixie
Leaving me with chem trails of glitter and
Magic to huff in irritation
Your left-over aura might be the reason
I can't detox from this contemplation
But I hope your wings continue to flutter
And land you on a petal that
Isn't frail enough for you to fall through
Like the one I offered when you fell into
My lap

I'll be rooting for you
Here's to you
Attract good fortune in abundance
But if you don't mind
Do it over there
So I won't miss you more than I should
Looking back at the past gets mad
Redundant

Manners Are Important

"The test of good manners is to be
able to put up pleasantly with bad ones." -
Wendell Willkie

There is a time and place for every
Attitude
But the one you've picked just now?
Will get the brakes beaten off you
Lower that tone!
Straighten your back
Be respectful.

Speak your opinions but remember
We have to get along at the end of
All this
Weigh your options
Do you want to be correct all the time?
Or do you want to be alive with secrets?

Knight In Rusty Armor

I know a good man is as
Rare as an undercooked steak
Or
Jimi Hendrix
With an acoustic guitar
But I can reassure your concerns
I don't expect anything
I'm shocked this is even happening
I can be satiated having a coffee
And listening to you telling me what
That cunt Samantha said in the office this
Morning
I know one half-decent man cannot
Sanitize the sooty violated lens you
Are obligated to view the world in
The image of your knight in shining armor
Has gone where the Easter Bunny and the
Tooth Fairy and the Chupacabra go

But you still deserve a knight
Maybe not a squeaky-clean knight
But a rustic
Occasionally dissociating knight
Who can't restore the hope you've lost
But can protect the hope you have left

Let It Rip

Back when the Nintendo Wii
Was peak technology
The kids on my block saved time
For each other
We had these spinning tops
From a show called "Beyblades"
We'd hold tournaments in the streets
Never giving a damn about who
Needed to get home to bring their
Groceries in or have their pre-dinner
Beer
We would bet on these tournaments
Cashless in hand we compromised
We bet with dares and promises
"I dare you to smash Ms. Sharp's mailbox
if I win"
We had a code to honor so
Ms. Sharp typically became livid after
The battle
"If I win you have to promise to let me
wear your new sneakers to school next week"
We had a code to honor so
The following week the entire cafeteria
Knew who won the most recent battle

See us kids all we had was our spinning
Tops and our word
We respected deals
We never scammed gypped or swindled
Each other
That was the only community
I ever felt heard my voice

Consider my desires
And gave me a fair fight for it
Those spinning top tournaments
Were democracy and capitalism at it's
Finest

Everyone worked for what they wanted
And we came to a consensus no matter
How much time we allotted another to
Advocate for
And no matter how many nail-biting
Hyperventilation inducing
Possibly friendship ending
Battles we had
We always found peace on the streets

Spiteful Adaptability

The gas prices are the highest when
I need a refill
My wallet asphyxiated from the
Excessive spending
It turned anorexic
I had to adapt out of spite
That's why you might
See me on my Razor scooter
Throwing eggs at your
Ducati
Jealousy can turn hate
Into your only hobby

I can't afford eggs anymore
But by the rules of relativity
I noticed you sold your Ducati
And can't get around

Boy, do I have
The perfect solution for you
I'll lend you my scooter
Rent it for $20 a ride
And with these due payments
All in due time
I can get your Ducati back
And take it for a test drive
Keep the scooter and the change
And here's some dust to chew on
Don't bother with revenge
By the time you get the eggs
I'll be long gone

Arpeggio

Dragging hands across my rib cage
Is more melodic than playing the
Harp
The "strings are thicker"
They make for heavy arpeggio's
So next time my
Calcium depletes and
Potassium secretes
Out of my ribs
It weeps
For SURE. You
Will see.

Aging Be Like…

When the
Ferocity and unforgiveness of
Age begins to display on familiar
Faces sagging
And you realize that you're
So far from the good
Old days that they've
Just become the
Old days
Nothing is more frightening
Than that

Individual Sidewalk Squares

The sidewalk square where
I earned my black eye
Appears contrite besides the line of

The sidewalk square where
I sauntered past the gun shots
Which pays homage to the line of

The sidewalk square where
I passed up the right of passage
Due to the line of

The sidewalk square where
My intelligence in-took some steroids
And caused the line of

The sidewalk square where
The term "genius" became a pseudonym
For the line of

The sidewalk square where
I earned my black eye
To be re-baptized

Forever Until Recently

Rudimentary trident taps
Skewered along the salacious
Sweats dripping over the spiky
Brow peering down
Down
The white tank top bared bravely by
Sinners eroding like cola carbonation
Hell-level sizzling
Forever Until Recently.

Yeah, enjoy that cloudy, rustic sauna
Spawn-camping impulsive, intrusive, intrinsic
"Character developments"
What troubles me is piggish
Children stacked in trench coats
Gourmandizing rifles and pistols
Acting like the repercussions are
"No big deal" Maybe it was
Forever Until Recently.

The history books tell tale of a time
When "reds" could've stolen your
White, and blue skies
Slurped through disintegrating paper
Straws. Those were
Not straws, but a telescope!
A telescope to study how
The extraterrestrials escaped
Repugnant nightmares all are
Enslaved to
Forever Until Recently.

Rudimentary trident taps
Now warmed up and oiled
Ready to feast
The sinners tax collector
Wouldn't worry about the unharmonious
Fears of our mutual evil
Unconcerned and patient
Watching us kill each other
Forever Until.........Well
That part is still going...

Ill-Behaved

I had a stint of shoving
Fortune cookies in people's corneas
Show punks their future
They called me the Silver Surfer
Of my day
I'd herald Armageddon
Uncontainable Contaminated
Ill-Behaved

Oh that's cute you
Get your best ideas in the shower?
And before you sleep?
I get my best quotes inside the car
Drag racing
Causing panic. Raking so many oats they
Assimilate into kaiju terrorizing states
Million-dollar babies abducting agriculture by the
Reigns
I'm so Ill-Behaved

My poems are Covid
They can't be washed away
Misfits make the best writers
We always have something to say
Out of our depth? Well
There's no such thing
When you're surfing galaxies
It's like a magnifying glass to dwarves
I zoom in on the gore
Log it, and pull a page like a rip cord
I'm a writer that grinds for more

But to most I'm just

Ill-Behaved

Krill

You want to be Romeo and Juliet?
That's a tragedy…I would've hoped
You wanted this to work out
And live happily/
\Ever after a hug you get chills
Like a construction drill?
I'm the krill if you're the whale/
\You eat me up in conjunction
With all others like me
You choose to brood from the top
Of the food chain/
\I was out of my depth I
Wish I knew before you cast
Me out like a reel
So I kept on swimming
As a lonely krill
That's all I ever sea
So that's all I get to be

Pending Text Message

I heard your dad died I meant
To   check up on that but
I   figured you didn't remember
Who   I was I was
That guy from a few years ago that
Made   You smile occasionally you
Evidently could tell we both
Needed it   I just thought I
Would reach out and say hey
Condolences   Have a great summer
Merry Christmas and
Whatever happens in August
We might meet again soon
We can hit that one park like we used to
Drag each other around bedraggled
And wound
Improv a scene where we never
Parted ways and I'll learn about

What you've been through since
And you can ask me
What's good and
I'll freestyle a few fibs
It's all in due time
Get me back when you can
Peace and love to ya.

Shouts Out To You

Hey kid,
I haven't seen you since the
Incident. No need to beat yourself up,
You tried to overcompensate and
Got a taste of the rubble
The boys clowned you.
Had you feeling red hot like the red
Dot was on your nose
A tale as old as time old
As reindeer in the snow
So what your little crush saw?
We all have our faults, if she
Slips through the cracks
She was meant to fall
You're still young. The more you let
This choke you up you'll suffocate
Take a deep breath and dust off
Those jeans
Cringe ain't nothing to worry about
Keep being yourself, king
If those bullies don't lay off
Ask me for some help
I'll bust out the belt
Teach you how to stand up for
Yourself
How to explain the way those
Boys look exactly like the elves
And when they gather outside they
Leave Santa's toys on the shelf.
You're a giant little bro
Don't think acting will save you
Enough is enough

Let it be
Flushed cheeks are temporary
You feel me?
Cringe ain't nothing but astonishment
And fear of someone being who they
Are.
Shouts out to you kid.
-Big Bro

Sunscreen

I feel free whenever I have sunscreen
On
And the waves crash
Out   And the sun notices I haven't
Been cooked not even
Pre-heated in fact it looks like I'm
Fresh out the womb
My wrist color matches the
Sea foam combing the shore

I feel free whenever I have
Sunscreen on and the ocean and
The sky become conjoined twins
The boats shimmy down the horizon
If I really wanted I could try
To swim out there

I feel free whenever I have sunscreen
On
And my friends get my back
We run we tackle we sip we smoke
The fun doesn't end until we can't
See
Then we rejoin society
Escaping to the oasis I
Feel so free when I put on
Sunscreen

On The Pot

I'm tryna piss and this
Fly keeps buzzing near my
Exposed body it's the most
Action I've gotten in a
While and I'm just tryna
Ride out the clock at work
So I can get paid
And go home

I remember all the heavy lifting that's
Now caused my back to ache I
Swipe at the fly

I remember my bi-weekly paycheck is
7 days away I
Swipe at the fly

I remember I have to wait at least a year
To get to be considered for a bonus or raise I
Swipe at the fly

I remember I clock out in 19 minutes
And a knock on the door said I need to
Piss or get off the pot I
Ignore it and
Swipe at the fly

Cool Matters

Cool is respect
Envy
Everyone wants to be cool
And it matters

It shouldn't
But it does
People will smoke to look cool
Speak obscene to look cool
Tote guns to look cool
Anything to breed more of themselves
If you want better habits
Make decency cool
Make solidarity cool
Turn it to a trend if you have to
All change has to be exciting these days
Nothing excites the masses like
A cool trend to gain respect

Cool matters

Be Still Thy Cries

You were a geyser when I found you
I coddled you to a fountain
And eased you to a faucet
Be still now
You're safe and there is no
Earthquake it's just your thighs shaking
And the avalanche is only me
Catching you in my arms policing the
Way you breathe
Be still now
You're safe and there is no
War
It's only the screaming neighbors next
Door
They are still in the transitional period
Of geyser to fountain
We are beyond them
Be still now
You're safe and there is no
Ambush on the way
It's just the stampeding herd of your
Loved ones coming to rescue
You in ways I
Cannot
Be still now
You're safe and there is no
Tears to cry
For the rest of the night

Dust

I wanted to read some poetry
I puffed the dust off my most recent
Bukowski purchase and plopped it on
My bed ripe for the reading plucking
Pages with the ferocity of a coked up
Harp player
As I sit down to read my phone lights
Up with a rare but enticing text
Notification
As I open the viral video my friend sent me
I pull out the Cheetos bag I was saving
For my free hand during my reading time
The longer the video plays the
More Cheeto dust I have on my fingers
And the dust once stuck to my Bukowski
Book dissipates in disappointment
I'm accumulating the lesser dust
And when I join the dirty particles

Myself post-cremation my remains
Will float and bob past open windows
Watching all the other people ignoring
The half-read books on their beds
And the off-white pages inside will grow
Lighter from the absence of attention
And I will be as disgusted as the
Passed away readers that resurrected as
The dust in my newly purchased Bukowski
Book

Cough Drop Wrapper

The evening is quiet enough for
Me to trick myself into thinking I am
Not doing well
The Rottweiler is barking through dry wall
Delivery drivers have started their week
Before the week has started for the
                                Recipients
The doctors and security guards never
See a week cease

I have decided I am not well I
    Will write about this to feel better

I can hear the football game downstairs
    The crowd in the TV is chanting
REF YOU SUCK
                            Louder than the Rottweiler
I grab my pen notebook and my throat
    Begins to feel like it's wrapped in
        Chain Mail armor
I grab a honey lemon cough drop

The wrapping on the cough drop
        Correctly assumed
I wasn't doing well there are adages
    On the wrapping like
IT'S YOURS FOR THE TAKING
        KEEP GOING
TOUGH IS YOUR MIDDLE NAME
I chuckle at the corporations trying to
    Ease some humanity into my night
But as always

The Rottweiler swears louder
And the refs' feedback is louder
Than that

Average Open Mic Night

I once saw a comedian lose
His mind on stage
It was one of the weaker bits honestly…
He wasn't cognizant of how he could
Spin that numbing anger into
An avant-garde masterpiece
He just blankly lost
His mind on stage
He ransacked the props knocked
The fake potted plant off
The platform and erupted a foul
Stream of aggression on innocent
Audience members trying to support
The local comics
After the show he stormed outside and
Hopped and stomped the ground like he

Wanted a sinkhole to swallow our city
The comedian chucked beer bottles and
Smashed a side mirror off the club owners
Car and it was funnier than the jokes
He told
The police tried to detain him but
He finessed the handcuffs from the cop
And linked him to a light pole and pantsed
The poor pig who
Then got so upset he started crying which
Was acclaimed as the funniest
Set of the entire night

It was here I learned the mad houses
Are just private open mic venues

And you can get the same entertainment
By spending $5 for a
5-minute set
That you'd find behind heavy medication
And insular living

The insane asylum is all around us
The only problem is
Sometimes the patients don't land
The punchlines on their first try

Some Mantras For You To Steal

I am the volcano that erupts
Only when provoked
I am the hand that feeds the mouth
Of the ones that say thank you
I am the gold plating on the fake chain
That makes it look real
I am the country-wide road trip taken
After the terminal diagnosis
I am the oppositions failed attempts
I am the single blade of grass that
Survives the lawnmower
I am rock to scissors
I am paper to rock
I am scissors to paper
I am the bullet that ends the war
I am the water coming through the dam
I am the tap of the boxers gloves before
The championship fight
I am the scaffolding around the
Tower of Babel
I am the turned cheek to the
Backhanded compliment
I am the closed ear to the
Constant chastising
I am the antenna tuned to the
Undiscovered frequency
I am the distance between the
Sun and the moon
I am the final kiss of the one
You never wanted to lose
I am whatever I want whenever I want

Free Palm

With just one palm: I could secure
Your seat next to where I eat.
But with my free palm? Well, that's up
To me.
I could smack you upside the head
High five you for a joint applause
Carry the plate I'd pass to you
Or drop it on the lawn
Pull your hand in for a smooch
Then throw it away in disaster
Predict your future through a bruise
Or wave goodbye as your impact prepares a brace
And all that is with my FREE palm. Be glad I
Don't use both.

Domesticate Invaders

My first day on this planet
They threw me a celebration
And ordered me some shots so strong
They had my
Neurons going like Times Square at night
Between fleeting glimpses of
My fuzzy stupor I drunkenly ascertained
How I'd found myself in a crowd so
Incredible
I knew I'd found my people
But they impress me so much that
I didn't feel like I

Belonged
So I do what any self-respecting invader
Would do. I adapted. Played to their
Empathy and the once intimidating group
Of role models stooped to my level.
We became equals and I knew I had them.
I had successfully domesticated this
Planet I hadn't seen a
Sixteenth of a fraction of yet
I don't assume anybody is cool
I let them do that to me

Real Change

Real change
Welcome back
This pass through the toll will cost
You one friend of mine
Take a friend I've spent the past year with
Learning about their fear's aspirations
Hot takes and cold daps

Real change
You owe me
Company
You owe me a new star not to replace
The previous shine but to illuminate the
Space adjacent to it and
Reveal as much to me as the star
I traded you for
Make today an auspicious day
For both my old friend and new star

Real change
When our friends move away
They are your responsibility
You do not take from us
You borrow
Know this next time
You decide someone needs to
Move away

Early Signs Of Aging

We're all old souls
I started losing hair at 22
Burdened with microscopic follicles
Concerned about preserving my youth

I cannot stop age
But my brush can fend it off
For just a little longer
I can keep the slow creep of
Sore joints and spores
On my teeth
At bay. Dormant. At peace

I cannot stop age
But my brown hairs can learn to
Get along with my grey hairs
They can divvy up their property

On my head properly
And when they embrace arms like
A barrel of monkeys
It might invite others to think I'm wise

I cannot stop age
I can hardly even confront it
But that spotted double mirror
And poor fluorescent bathroom lighting
Reminds me our days are numbered
So I'll live it up while I can
And sprint like a track star until
I'm bound to a wheelchair
And roll even faster than my
Legs could carry me

I cannot stop age
But I CAN make it an excuse
To let loose

Uncomfortably Smooth

There's no more tactile things
I feel so disconnected from
Technology
I write by touching my pad
And the words pop up
I don't get to experience the
CLACK CLACK CLACK
That all the big writers talk about
I don't feel like a chemist in a
Lab I
Feel like a bum playing with
Rubber slabs
The new commandments will be on
Those   That's what creating is now
Most things are smooth
There's no divots anymore
No bumps
No gaps
Just smooth

"It Gets Better"

But I worry I don't have
The patience for
Delayed gratification
Especially if
Victory now
Will make you proud
And jealous
Internally

Why can't it be better
Now?

Laughing + Crying

Sometimes when you cry your
Mouth
Splits open kind of
Like it does when
You smile

That was the first hint
That joy and suffering
Are long-quarreling lovers

The second hint is the eye squint
The third is the hitched-breath tempo
Laughing and crying

Are one in the same
I feel like no one realizes how
Unfortunately hysterical that is

Everybody Wanna Be A Poet

Until the gargantuan gizzard of
Dumbfoundedness digests
The last observation they had left
And the well runs dry

With a bucket to play hacky sack with
Conjuring the comet that killed
The dinosaurs to trace a quote

So poignantly numb they can gaslight
Some commoner into coughing up two cents

Many wield stingy orifices, however.

So the poet resorts to violence
Yanking plastic bags of dismembered notions
Rabid electrolytes that poets consolidate
Are not worthy of anyone's haunches
Being a poet is more than a quiet storm

It's rotating rehabilitation
Polyester and wool straitjackets
The tinnitus-like ringing of
Reclaimed beauty repackaged for anthemic plights

Spellling Errors

I sprinkle typos
In my poems sometimes
So everyone knows I'm
Not pretentious, I'm pretending
I'm not superior, I'm superstitious
So when I write on the wall
I spell every word wrong
And when others read it out loud
Blind people think I have an
Accent when I talk
I'm not perfect. The red lines on my
Word document know it
My work is so poorly written AI couldn't
Decode it
But I like it
Human mistakes like spellling errors
Are about to go away. The robots are
Making way. You'll miss these typos one
Day

Old Bitch In The Left Lane

The construction workers are slap boxing
Their wheels frustrated
They won't make it to the worksite on time
Because this old bitch in the left lane
Is causing all this traffic

An expecting mother is trying to clench
Her torso so her baby isn't born in a
Honda
But she's worried it might happen
Because this old bitch in the left lane
Is causing all this traffic

An intoxicated driver is counting his
Breaths
Doing his best to escape the dizziness
The traffic is as sluggish as he is
And he's thankful he has a moment to
Reacclimate his mind with the road
Thanks to this old bitch in the left lane

This old bitch in the left lane
Hands shaking trembling like she's
Rolling a thousand dice
She's just trying to get to her exit
She's almost there when she looks in
Her rearview mirror to see the astonishingly
Long line of cars creeping along
For a split second she feels guilt
But shrugs it off remembering how hard
It was to live this long
She's earned the right to be

The old bitch in the left lane

The Past Stays Put

Bask
In the photos we took
Appreciative of the arms wrapped around
Each other's shoulder blades
Before we knew we weren't exempt from
The hourglass that deteriorated
Spry healthy children
Overtime to middle aged lethargic
Rat fucks

Fawn
Over the war re-enactments we
Orchestrated in the valley
Flipping the script with ray guns and
Fatal injuries you can recover from
No paramedics needed
No fund but left with some lump sums
Bloated

Relish
In the gunk sleeping under our fingernails
That moved in after each football tackle
Game of tag and duck duck goose
Inadvertently replicated with
The gunk reluctantly napping under our
Fingernails from burying grisly secrets
Bodies hopes and the fireflies caught in
Our mason jars

Justifying The Pain

I wish I could skip to the part where
This all turns into a silly memory

A story to add to my repertoire
Of ice breakers
Horror stories are still
Entertaining

I appreciate a tragic comedy
And most parties do too
Every new setback I face
Is an excuse to lighten the mood

Nothing happens TO you
It all happens FOR you.
That's what they tell me
After my stories end

Holiday Season

Forks and knives volleyed over our
Hundred-dollar ham
We invade each other's privacy
Over the processed cranberry sauce
Judgmental side eyes skip by the
Macaroni and cheese

The holiday season is a test
Of turmoil to many
But once you decipher the patterns:
What sets who off
And you can outline the perimeters
Of the sensitive subjects and sore spots
Learn how to behave and restrain
Unfiltered thoughts fleeing the brain
That's when holiday fear
Turns into holiday cheer

Unholy Offspring

Backhanded backstabs
Fool me once fool me twice
We come from the same place
Yet the cavity that spurted
Us out seems to favor
Diversity
One of us has become
The unholy offspring
And although I can't be certain
I like to think it's not me
However…

Oblivious, Over It

You couldn't understand my side of
The story so I projected
The rage I felt
In every stale belch
And let my pent-up rage
Waft towards you and singe
Your eyebrows off
Now I can't tell HOW upset you are

I told you I wasn't great at this
And that I'd try my best
But not for nothing you could
Communicate directly instead
Of surreptitiously whispering
And shushing me-like fuck
We're on the same team!

But you don't feel safe enough to
Know I won't do what those
Deplorable violators did to you
I can only save you to a certain extent
As oblivious as I am
I can lead you to safety but
I cannot make you feel safe
So run out if you must
Do not suffer just to be polite to me
Just tell me straight up
And I'll get over it
Or if you want you could leave without
A trace
I'd be too oblivious to notice anyways

Campsite Chaos

Since I found my
Way   Back to the campsite
I've been telling people the anecdotes
To all the new all-natural un-cured scars
That I attained while I was lost
But   I can't even remember
Which parts were real
I wouldn't know if that beady
Red streak
On my leg is poison ivy
Or if I stepped in a bushel of berries
It might be the former
Because the tent we sleep in has
Grown a mouth
And eyes   The crickets nearby
Chirps sound like pianos and banjos

And all my friends' heads turned into
Copies of me
This must be a solipsistic day dream!
I look to the DreamWorks-logo-looking
Moon to recalibrate
There's pterodactyls swirling in mid-air...
I'm losing my damn mind; I'm tweaking off poison ivy
For sure

My friends usher me to a chair
Force water down my gullet   And
Tend to the ambiguous   Red streak
By rubbing small alcohol pads on my calf
And I looked at the pterodactyls in the sky
And all the clones of myself

I think "This is a sick way to die"
The tent starts talking to
Me   The tent tells me how lucky I am
To hallucinate with such an aesthetic
And I slump back in my chair whistling
To the sounds of the instrumental crickets
And I enjoy the chaos while it lasts

Abstract Art, You Are

It's always cracked me up the way
Diagnosing psychological illnesses
Is essentially up for interpretation.
Like we're personified works of abstract
Art. We walk up with tension so palpable
You could cut it with a crayon
And someone takes that crayon and
Colors in and out of the lines
They bring all your abnormalities to light
Your little idiosyncrasies are lathered in
Primary and secondary colors

Jagged around some edges
Smooth around others
My oh my
What an abstract work of art you are
And after this deliberation you
Walk around and more people look at you.
They interpret you as well
You look like a brand new work of art
To each and every person
My oh my
What an abstract work of art you are

After The Battle Quips

I get flashbacks
Of the patchy, mowed grass
Wiping your pilling lips
As you bled faster than you could quip
I admired so strongly
That even after trading your life
With a gaping cavern in your side
You found the time
To joke about the mess of humanity around us
The conversation was so refreshing
I would've forgotten we fought
If not
For
Your
Final
Quip

What If Heaven Denies Us?

Us speedy sheep in search of the
Blitzkrieg
Autonomous bombs colossus size
The herald of catastrophe

We won't have nukes in heaven NO
Power in artillery NO buttons to push

We can make a case in words that
REPEAT REPEAT REPEAT
AGAIN AND OVER AND CONSTANT

We will have words wherever we go

Homeless Painter

This homeless prodigy down
Town turns blocks like Tetris
Trying to make a dime off of
Some paintings that look better than
What is being passed today as
"Contemporary" art
He's an old man. He's amassed many
Paintings. Each more nuanced and daring
Than the previous

I never have the money to buy a painting
But I feel so guilty. That old man
Is one home short of being us
An aspiring artist capable of changing
The game. Overlooked and shoved into
The underpass

Should the day come where I'm writing
Poems on backs of missing pet posters
With expo marker I'd still be proud
But do my efforts come with enough pride
The pride chock full of all vitamins
I need?
Will every body of work I body
Be enough to get me to the next
Body of work?

Maybe A Dumb Statement

I'd rather live a lack-
Luster life built from
My own volition
Than a great life
Gifted from someone else
No matter the intention
I'm grateful to be a
Beneficiary, but I'm
Even more appreciative
Of the twigs my nest
Consist of

Violence

I heard someone say
"I don't understand how some people could be
So cruel!" …Really?
You ever over-drafted on a bagel
Then got hit in the kidneys?
You'd wanna do something about it
Huh?
What if someone hurt your true love
And football punted your kid?
You'd go ballistic
Huh?
Somebody used your grandmas' ashes
To make soil for a tree
Without permission and her nightgown
Gets turned into leaves?
…Huh?
I take a brick to your TV
Then tie you to a chair and force you
To watch me steal your belongings?
…Huh?!
Fill your car with wasps and rip the
Handles off then get your car towed
Because I claimed you were hogging my spot?
Huh…

Violence is abundantly necessary
It works wonders
Or maybe it has the POTENTIAL to
I wonder…

I Used To Be Beautiful

I used to be beautiful
Everyone would tell me and I never
Believed them
I would tell myself they were lying and
Trick myself into thinking I looked
The way I do now

I used to be beautiful
Back when my gums and hairline weren't
Petrified of the center of my face
I'd smile in the sun and it wouldn't
Uncover
Some wretched grotesque secret
Some secret that shows I'm not the same

I used to be beautiful
I looked so incredibly beautiful
And now
I look like I USED to be so incredibly
Beautiful

I used to be beautiful
And maybe I still am now
Maybe I'm tricking myself into
Thinking I've already lost as much as
I'm going to lose later down the line

Americans Don't Read

THEY only want the
Cliff notes so they **SKIM**
THROUGH elaborate novels
Furnished with lessons only **BOOKS**
Can teach
THEY listen to the chatter and fill the
Blank parts they **SKIM**
THROUGH look at the reports
There's countless **ARTICLES**
THEY show the statistics
In reference to the gradual decline kids
Are being raised to **SKIM**
THROUGH the most prevalent tales
Glossing over iconic characters relatable
Issues and personality-altering **POEMS**

A Different Kind Of Annoying

A throbbing demand to get out of the
House
Is excusable. The ruckus running rampant
You HAVE to vacate from that zone
But there isn't always a tranquil
Atmosphere. Some hidden oasis
Waiting for you and only you to visit
Sometimes you can't get away from
ALL the annoyances
So you pick your battles
A scathing group of familiars
Can be softened with a rowdy sports bar
And this yelling ejected from tens of tens
Of overly masculine men and women
Can be comforting for those who need
To get away   But not be alone
Sometimes you don't need quiet   You need
A different kind of annoying
The kind that isn't aimed at you
The kind that just is

Just A Little Something

I am not who I was when you first met
Me yet you treat me like I am.
You must miss who you were back then
Even more
Than you miss
Who I used to be

Juggernaut

What can I say?   I can't top feeling
Invincible
That's gotta be my favorite drug
Feeling so invincible that you start racing
Nobody at full speed
Bashing through walls with the technique
Of the Juggernaut

Breaking down breaking down that's all
I do.
I break down bashfully
With arrogance
And room for improvement

I can always be better
I cannot be stopped
I'm the Juggernaut
And that's my burden to tote around
That's the special curse I was assigned
Being
The Juggernaut

Busy Night

I reserved this bunker for myself tonight
I'm going to summon some people
To haunt me
For fun
The spirits gawk at
My
Broiled verbs
And
Malnourished adjectives
And they tell me
How close I am to joining them
Last week they told me
I was getting better
(Which is not good for what I'm trying to do)
So they cut me some slack
And gave me approximately 4 1/8
Lackluster days to redirect me
To the point of no return
But I didn't anguish like usual
The spirits notice I'm becoming
"A resilient and respectful piece of shit"
And they tell me they can't haunt me
Anymore
I'm becoming a better man
At the cost of losing plans
Now I have to spend tomorrow night
Being bored bare and better than ever
So if anyone is free and
Emotionally intelligent
Hit me up.

Which Is Better

All of my heroes
Died young
Or aren't real
Which is better?

Good deeds get punished
And villains get money
Which is better?

Some people cope
Others have fun
And stay ignorant
Which is better?

Some writers write
Some writers perform
Some writers post
Which is better?

2 Loud 2 Many Questions

222 thoughts
Removed from anything corporeal
Trying to shed stress from
111 varied sources in real time
(So VERY SLOWLY)
Still the suppressed sound collage
Moves around me like a grey cloud in that
Cartoon made for Saturday mornings
I'm watching while I eat my
Food battered with
The same damn questions:

"How are you? Do you need anything? Are you sure?
Why not? Can you repeat that? What's wrong?
Why won't you talk to me? Are you hungry?
What did you eat today? Want some more?
Are you thirsty? Do you want some water?
Are you sure? Are you positive?
Are you a hundred percent positive?
Are you sure you're a hundred percent positive?"

That bland flavor of question
That keeps conversation going
For no good reason
Every time someone puffs out their chest
Conjuring another fucking question
The impending doom
Creeps slower than
A server offering hors d'oeuvres like
Jesus Christ!

"Can't you tell I'm tired and don't wanna be bothered?!
How

Dismissive do I have to be before you take the hint?!
How's that for asking questions?!
Am I bothering you now?! How do YOU like it?!
Is this what you wanted?!
You wanted me to answer your damn questions right?!
What's wrong?! Why're you upset now?!
Was it something I said?! Can you shut up?!
Can you leave me alone?!"

Eventually the barrage of questions
Subsides
And I am finally alone
Alone filled with rancid exasperation
Irate as fuck
My head is a burlap sack of
Vexing aggravation
And I am sitting
Sitting there alone pissed with no
Way to let it out
And I wish I had someone to
Talk to about the things that anger me
But the only one who cared...
I just cursed them the fuck out
And they have left me
Alone
Because I asked them
...

...

...

You Ever Have...

One of those moments when
You
SCREAM
With the intention
Of emancipating your
Mind from your brain
But all it does
Is remind you
Why you keep
Your stupid mouth shut?

When The Honey Moon Falls

You know we could've been something
Special
But we get too enthralled and used
Up all our love at once
Now our supply
Is bone dry
We ignored the truth for long enough
 But could I get one more
 Kiss before I dip in the
 Mist to fight off the horde?
And defend the grains I
Graze, desecrate, search, and explore?
Since after this I won't
See you anymore…
Keep the heartstrings I gave you
And create some new chords

Write a lullaby in my memory
Play it before you sleep
To summon me in your dreams
I know I'm obsessed with fantasy
You'd prefer I stay in reality…
Stability has never been on our side, honey
And as I teeter across the line of
Scrimmage and the tirade I face sprints
At me with the speed of Apollo 10
The syrupy honeymoon falls at the same
Pace
And with my backside to you
You really see me for the first time
I don't dare look back at you
I'm too afraid to besmirch the
Indefectible façade you tricked me with

So I leave you…
And so, I leave to you:

Safety and possibility
May you find someone who will
Stay by your side and shield you
Rather than run off to the epicenter
Of trespassers and defenders
And betray the protector you thought
Me to be
Before the honey moon fell

Unfair Cycles

When the turtle returns to the
Sandy shore to lay eggs galore
Does it remember all the gore
Their brothers and sisters
Fell victim to before?
And get PTSD from the seagulls that
Swarmed and ate them whole?
And does the turtle feel guilt
Knowing most of it's
Babies might meet the same fate?

Haunted House

Lost in a haunted house
Doors creaking leaking storm drains
Leaving the couch doused
It's too dark
I find a candlestick under the arch
Marked where a skull and bones hang
Spotting a pack of matches
I ignite and light
In the tepid erratic warm I'm
Frightened from two fangs
Connected to the frown of
My grandfather passed away
Looking as sapped and sheet-white
As he looked on that
Fateful day

"I haven't seen you in a while
Bud…I missed you when I was still awake"
I couldn't believe my eyes
I finally could tell him all that I had to say
"I'm so sorry I left and never came back,
I was carving my own
Path. Just trying to make the most of a life
You never had! A life you gave up for
Me…It was all in your best interests!"
He said

"Dearest grandson, I know. I've been watching and
Reviewing all you did. I went back in time
And became the will you
Needed to live.
I possessed the lady that

Paid for your bagel when you were broke, I
Had to make sure you ate.
I was the first snowflake that melted onto
Your nose, it was the only way I could
Become part of you again.
I was every rat that scurried across
Your toes, just to make sure you were alert
And aware in that city alone.
And I was the darkness in between
Your eyes every time you blinked
So you could catch a glimpse of the
Original smile I'd flash to lull you
To sleep"

I cried. "I'm sorry I couldn't make it back to you
Like you always hoped. To talk to you one last time
Before you dropped into that casket
Looking the way you do now"
He wiped my tears away
And I figured it was the opposite effect of
That first snowflake he became to reunite
With me
And he said in that voice I've adhered to
Since he first held me
"Oh beautiful boy, were you not listening?
You'll see me everywhere you go
It doesn't matter what I look like.

And suddenly the house wasn't haunted
It just had some good company
That only I could see
And with one ethereal hug
The drains stopped spilling
And the couch was dry
And we sat and talked

Until the candle went out
As did my grandfather
With it

Common Courtesy

I stay in the gutters when I smoke

In neighborhoods

I keep my ash off their driveways

Because the last time that happened

Old man Gary sicced his dog

On me

And I had to put the bitch down

But I let the dog live

The dog didn't seem too disturbed by this

So, no harm no foul

Same Old Same Old

I come down the stairs
Like an ogre learning how to dougie
Greeted with the repugnant visual of
Orange
Juice with so much pulp
It's reverted back to a solid
I ate my drink and ran for the bus

I lugged myself up the steps
Like I was a man of steel
I tried to hike to the back of the bus
But
I was tripped by the rebellious dick
That was on-and-off with my
One true love
(Before I had met my OTHER true loves)
I fell like I was a man of steel

In Algebra we received a pop quiz about
A lesson we had started yesterday and I
BOMBED in a manner more gnarly than
Any of the famous bombings that
Probably came to your mind just now
I got the lowest grade of the
Entire class

At lunch I got my money stolen by
The rebellious dicks friend so
My buddy shared with me his butter
Sandwich

The bell rings with prowess not unlike
Paul Revere warning all them about the

British
And on the bus ride home
Nobody trips me
I'm not hungry
I've gotten my revenge, I thought to myself
I win again

British
And on the bus ride home
Nobody trips me
I'm not hungry
I've gotten my revenge, I thought to myself
I win again

Invisible Cruelty

All this free-range hostility
    Weaponized by

    Crooked cops removing
    Body cams
    Dragonflies idiotically trusting a
    Praying Mantis
    A young girl brutalized by her mothers
    Friend

    All this free-range hostility
    Materialized from

Playing hide n go seek with food stamps
    The demanding removal of rainforests
    A divorced man's first night in a motel

    All this free-range hostility
        Redeemed via

    Gang wars unknowingly representing
    World wars
    Middle school egos in mahogany dictator
    Chairs
    Fire as far as the entire head could
    Comprehend

    All this free-range hostility
    And it still hasn't defeated us

Final Talk

I remember my buddy Colton from
Elementary school
And the last time we ever spoke
After the last day of fifth grade
Waiting for his little brother
We stood on a wooden bridge
Moldy, nasty, rank, it smelled like
Excrement
He yapped on about his
Recurring dream of going to war
And getting in knife
Fights like a badass
At 11 he was convinced that was
His purpose and he confided in me
That he was thrilled to see violence
We knew we'd never see each other again
And it wasn't a big deal
He asked me what I wanted to do
And I gave him an answer so
Ludicrous it impressed him
He seemed to believe I'd make it
Come to fruition
If I told him what I'm up to now
I'd let him down
His brother finally came
And we hugged goodbye
It was the most innocent hug
That's ever been
We parted ways
And it wasn't a big deal

Respect Your Elders

I wish I was Bukowski
With the romance of Plath
The experience of Hemingway
The inventiveness of Shakespeare
The darkness of Poe
The light of Whitman

Every writer wants to be the torch passer
But if you don't study the greats then it
                              Won't matter.
I try to funnel their prose into
                    My own habits
And all I get is blasphemous
                Slop
Smelling like a wet moose
Cruel and unusual
Words dismount off the pages
And stick to my nostrils

And they all look down upon me
"Look at him!   Look at him!"
They look amongst each other
"Remember when we used
        To write trash like that?"

The Comfort Song

I hug you once it's love
I hug you twice it's to block out
Your adversary
I hug you three times it's levity

Don't hesitate to tell me
You need me
People just want a savior
They can see
The injured need aid
And gentle community

I hug you once it's love
I hug you twice it's to block out
Your adversary
I hug you three times it's levity

Although I can't be your bedroom
I'll make you feel at home
And be the place you want to go
When you have nowhere else to go

I hug you once it's love
I hug you twice it's to block out
Your adversary
I hug you three times it's levity

What's everybody so stressed for?
When we've all been here before
There's no original disasters
We'll never run out of laughter

I hug you once it's love
I hug you twice it's to block out
Your adversary
I hug you three times it's levity

Anti-Fuel

You've come so far running away
From what you despise
You've grown so tall a bright glare
Censors your cynical stale eyes
And you've still got so much more to
Get away from

Would you like to know why you're still
Unhappy? Because you abuse yourself
With motivation
All you do to change is escape
Your progress is tainted
With the regret of yesterday
You still have a quarter tank left
But it's filled with Anti-Fuel

It's gonna wreck you when you burn out
With nothing more to perfect
But you'll still feel
Incomplete

I Was One Of Them Once

A leak in the homogeneous diaspora
Bent over and gross
Mothers shooing their children away
Like I was the nucleus of all disease

I was one of them once

Miscellaneous and unimportant
Also unincumbered
Laying on the ground like a shrimp
No responsibility
Nibbling
Bits of cork stuck in my teeth from
A bottle of hot
Chardonnay I found outside
Half-drunk like myself

I was one of them once

Hacking up
Phlegm
Mumbling
          "Amor fati"
To myself
While fathers guard their children
Like they didn't want their kids
To learn they could be just like me
If they try hard enough

Black Cat In Ohio

I crossed a black cat
Gave him his bad luck back
He got cat-napped and was scooped
Up sagging like a
Plastic bag full of Campbells soup

He got taken by the incest twins
    Ohio visitors who came down in the
    Summer
They liked the beaches and the locals
The beaches were a change of pace
The locals bred familiarity
    (Which was the incest twins forte)
    They took the black cat back
        Home to Ohio

The incest twins came back the next
Summer with a trash bag as black
As the cat and said
"Here's your cat back! He's tuckered out
From all the catnip, he's only taking a
Cat nap!"
I said "What did y'all do to him while
Y'all were gone?"
"Oh, we played games to see who can
Drink the most gasoline, shot at him
With BB's and nailed his tail to a tree!"
I said "Those three things took y'all a
Whole year?"
They said "We woulda finished the games
Sooner but he kept passing his bad luck
Back to us! We couldn't give him gasoline
Cuz the prices went up, the BB gun

Jammed whenever we had him in the
Scope, and the tree branches weren't
Sturdy enough!"
They handed me the bag and pranced
Along to find more tantalizing cats
To subject to their heinous games
I looked at the bag and said
"See that? That's called KARMA
                              Cat-Nap..."

Untitled

In my cubicle depraved
Floundering in misery for no reason
And I can't focus due to the
Frenzied   Swath
Of employees talking about their
Weekend plans and what countries
They would've visited if they
Didn't have to use their last batch of
PTO   To go to the dentist
                    I go to the bathroom
Expressionless and bored of
All the reasons I'm sad
And I stare at the roll of
Toilet paper that feels like
Mini lawn mower blades
When I wipe
And the sadness gets so redundant
That I start thinking about how
Nice Switzerland looks
Or how Jamaica seems so enjoyable
And I set a reminder on my phone
To brush my teeth before I go to bed
Tonight

Typecast

I'm becoming known for my
Vices they grip twist and dip
It feels too good to quit
Purified lifestyles are myths
What doesn't kill you
Only adds to the script
No need for abolition
Addiction is contradiction
I'm typecast as the doomed one
The false Gods well-behaved son
I'm a citizen's arrest in sheep's clothes
Woven cotton stained with rum

I'm offered treats non-stop
They expect the tricks later
It's not good when goodie-bags
Turn you into the party favor
It leads to a party foul
No gravitas   No bowing out
You only turn heads
That ask the same question
Like barn owls

A chipper mood can stitch a chip
To your shoulder
A chip off the ole' block
Vacate the streets with an odor
Keep in mind you can slow down now
Don't just wait until you're older

Talentless Writing

It's a bit too breezy
The A/C's bragging
I've been rhyming
   Riding   Wa
            ves
That earnest enigmatic
Touch
Which once pronounced me the leader
Of eight in a crowd
Wanted to explore its options.
Have a slut-phase
Zipping between other
Creatives like the unheated air
Equals: Me with the talent and vocabulary
Of a gift card with
Permanent marker over the redemption code
Paired well with a welt of
Indifferent effort

Water Your Garden

The other poets tell me to water
My garden so much that
I piss in their gardens out
Of spite
The other poets tell me to watch
My flowers blossom
I rip their flowers like a weave
Just to uproot their hard work
The other poets tell me to love
Even those who have wronged me
So I slashed their tires to drive
Them crazy in love with me
The other poets tell me to trust
My vision but all I see are the
Same anxiety attacks crystallized
In the same font
The other poets are better
The other poets get published
The other poets get likes
The other poets get reposted
The other poets water their gardens
The other poets flowers grow
The other poets notice mine wilt
The other poets are better

Time Out

I called a timeout.   Enter: Guardian Angel.
She fizzled into the air like
Confetti
Floating like placenta after
A water birth
She looked down on me
Novice as a virgin
"I'd be afraid if I were you. This is not an auspicious day.
It would behoove you to bemoan the debauchery in
Which you partake."

I told her majesty
"Try as I might to remain steadfast
On this janky voyage, I falter
In the name of education, ain't I noble for this?"

She goes
"You wish to be extolled for
Rolling belly up? Your arrogance will
Make way for a harpoon to skewer your guts"

I told her
"Stop rhyming! Clarify your message!
I'm bobbing alone in this mélange of shit will you
Save me or gaze upon me and spit?!"

She schools me
"You beg for a
Magnanimous being to aid and assist
I deal you advice, and I'm met with quips,
And hypocrisy?!
So snarky…this is why you walk alone
And fail so commonly!"

“APOLOGIES. Apologies”
I act right instantly

“My boy I cannot take you from this place
I am shackled to your feet. Your face is my
                                        Face.
I’m the bright side of your moon. I can influence
                              Your tastes
          And offer appetizers of alternatives
          But you must live with your mistakes”
          She dissipates

          The timer wakes up from its nap
          My bad temper got me in this
          My bad temper kicked her out
No matter. I’ll roll up my sleeves and earn
Her guidance again. I have 2 more
Time outs. I’ll show her what she’s missing
Her nerves, I’ll avenge.

About When I Went Missing...

Some days I go missing
In a fit of quiet protests
Like the man from
Tiananmen Square
I drop a bag
Just to pay the price
Come back 3 days
Later like the
Son of Christ
Thin and white
Like a grain
Of rice
I was stuck in
The sludge just
Fixing pipes
I had to run away
When it came to
Fight or flight
The answer I
Chose was Wright's
I must've spooked you
Gave you a little fright
Don't worry about what I do
Just know I'm now alright

Outside The Bar

Panic attacks from
These cheap thrills
It sorta gives me chills
I tremble and chatter
Staccato fills
Jittery like I took too
Many pills
My synapses snap
I'm going through
Aneurysm's
When I'm out
In public I
Panic different
Hope they don't see me
On camera in fetal
Position
I'm not trespassing I'm
Camping out
That's my
Prerogative let
Me go pout
It's my birthday
Circa right now
I'm a country mile
Way down south
My eyes are
Kettle cooked
I see sounds
It's isotopes in
The carbon coming
Out my mouth
Popping
Loud

They go like
BLAOW

What A Tremendous Shame

Oliver McCall is and was an
Excellent boxer
But most that know his name know
Him as the boxer that cried against Lewis

McCall broke down crying in '97
Defending a title he rightfully earned
But he was drugged out and stressed
In an eerily empowering daze
He scampered around the ring refusing to
Fight
He started crying
Crying Crying Crying
But he never backed down
He just cried through the punches
Cried and ducked.   Cried and blocked

He was sent to a mental hospital
And came back to win it all
The truest underdog of all the underdogs
But he isn't known for his comeback
He is known for crying against Lewis

I watch that video back sometimes and
Think: "Man, if he could've saved
His mental breakdown until AFTER the
Damn fight...he'd ONLY be known as
A great boxer."
What a tremendous shame it is to have
Such an immaculate image squandered
By the public cameos of your private life

A Poem From My Rookie Days

It's been too many days since I've
Written

I fear I am a fad
Or maybe I haven't slept enough

I haven't figured that one out yet
Everybody's going back to college

I haven't even cleaned my room
Everybody's going home early

It's been too many days since I've
Written

I've done much better than this
I'm just trying something new

Everybody's lowering their standards
I haven't even changed my mind

Everybody has a salary
I haven't had a chance to shower

Everybody can't meet up again
I haven't relied on something more

I've done much better than this
I'm just the derelict that broods

It's been too many days since I've
Written

Neon People

All the girls with pretty hair
Shine like highlighter on paper
Everything about this club is overpriced
But they look like they're worth a lot
They mean everything to everyone
And dance like they don't care

The bouncer tries to kick him out
But he's not congenial enough
To ignore a chance to spar in the wild
Because he knows:
Never miss an opportunity
To prove yourself and
Make someone look stupid

I am a little mix of both
The neon people and
The saturated ones
I'm visible and that's enough
I won't make a scene but I'm part of it

The Makings Of A Poet

In the ominous corner like the legends
Were. You hear these backstories of the
Greatest ones to ever do it and they
Always have distasteful sappy stories.
Lone mischiefs sneering at the worlds
Inability to catch up to a pioneer ahead
Of their time. So they trot whatever
Downtown metropolis they find
Themselves and embrace the filth
To keep themselves levelheaded. An icon
Of such stature, these are the makings of
A poet. They mumble humble shy
Semantics in a tenor so incomprehensible
They can only add to the horde of
Soon-to-be pieces of their generation.
Until they remain in the corner as
A sordid has-been who has never been
Anything before.

Lost Once Again

I only ever try my best
To give others something tangible
But the slot machine took my $20
And I lost the power spin
Once again. Looks like I lost once again.

I only ever spread love
Even if I get none back
But this one girl took my early 20's
And I forgot to get my hoodie back
Once again. Looks like I lost once again.

I only ever write enough
To impress my fountain pen
But the algorithm snuffed me out
And my failed attempt is prominent
Once again. Looks like I lost once again.

I only ever stress about
The things that truly matter
But these flamboyant fuckass flexers
Remind me I'm missing out
Once again. Looks like I lost once again.

Poor Babies

For sale: Baby shoes
Buy one get one half off
Severed ties in the maternity ward
Just for the experiment
Mothers breastfeeding babies
High fructose corn syrup
And cleaning up their
Chin with bibs tacked with anthrax

Mice, Hen
And
Bison

All mourn the poor babies
Forced into labor
Unable to taste flavors
Grinding in the mines until they
Barf up a liver
Poor babies

Invisible Prodigies
(Conceived during a stagehand job)

The kids were monstrously talented
And no one heard them but I
And a couple parents
In the echoey theatre
Rickety and limber as if it were
Made of twigs
The little men mastered the brass
Section of instruments and
I was lucky enough to be paid
Decently adequate money
To listen to them craft their sound

It was the greatest show one could
Hope to see for free
A young prodigy mid origin story
Unbeknownst to the world now
Practicing prodigies
Need
To stay invisible
And pop out with a surprise and pizazz
Like the brass jazz notes they play

Parasocial Relationship

Art connects you spiritually
The artist is your new messiah
Connection is the most overbearing
Addiction
  But that screen ain't your friend
      Don't turn up the volume
And mouth along to conversations
      Too good for your input

        There's an influx of loneliness
        Folks won't leave their homes again
        And when they do, retaliation
                More than likely ensues

So these stars become your friends
  Puppeteers' puppeteering you
Funny they're putting on a show
        But you think it stars you too
   Get outside   Touch grass
                That's a blast from the past
            Breathe some O2 instead
Of hot steam coming out the CPU

Backup Dancers

The swaying backup dancers
Slowly sashaying in the
Baking warm of orange light
Snapping their fingers
Rhythmically syncing to
Their two-stepping

The lounge singer is the only person
Of significance in here
He does his set blissfully crooning
The last time he was happy
The backup dancers are happier
Slithering like snakes
And the singer is
The snake charmer
And they work together
To generate enough elation
That every person in the club
Forgets about the anxieties
They have waiting in the applause
Breaks
The backup dancers
Patient and poised
Amplify the serenity
From their hair to the seams
Of their dresses in the orange light

She

She wanted me.
Was the rumor spread to get me inside
The bar and I knew it was a trap
From my well-meaning friends.
On the other side of the
LED sea
The most valuable treasure on two legs
I've seen this week
And by not pursuing her
I anoint myself as the special one
But my well-meaning friends whisk her
Away from her companion
And onto the stool next to me
And we talked
She mashed her life story into
Seven broken slurred breakdowns
I interjected some jokes
And I had to explain them.
She told some jokes and laughed at them
For me.
The talk was cut short and four sips
Later she was in the arms of a stranger
And it seared my lips shut
In the name of injustice
As if she owed me anything at all
Automatically, this went for my ego and
Diminished it into a wet paper towel
But the night was never about that
My worth isn't tied to a cute stranger
So I go back for sip five
And I feel how I did before she met me

Godzilla

No mercy for the bombs
Traumatizing grimaces for the
Radioactive wars
It's hard to get too invested when
It comes to these sci-fi debacles
What face does one make
When a shockwave comes at
The children?
Only Godzilla can save us at this point
The one monster on our side
He can tank the bombs and send
Them back from whence they came:
The bleach white den of scandals.
Where does one duck for cover when
The monsters attack each other?
When all in the blast radius disintegrates
Only Godzilla can save us at this point

Put The Fries In The Bag

"Yes yes I've been there gang
Grinding grueling hours
Before the big break
Praying that every time you clock out
You see the phone ring
From a call that couldn't reach you earlier
In the day
Saying you're next up
No amount of praise is a surefire thing
But the flame in your heart prevails
All the same
Through the ridicule you face
Young and curmudgeonly
The resentment rises like
Water from a bidet
But no one to take it out on
There's no one to blame
Except yourself and the way you define
Acceptance in the game
Who cares? It's nefarious anyways
The penultimate goal should be
Stable funds in the bank
The main goal should be hard work
Mixed with a couple breaks-
But enough of this pretense
Just put the fries in the bag, okay?..."

String Theory

I've been aware of the world around me
Before I could even remember
But I've only started to understand it now.
When you pay attention you notice that
Everything's connected.

Like one long breeze blows
Through us

Tagging each person within range
I think string theory is real
We all pull each other's strings
And play the eccentric enticing entrancing
Sounds that form together into
Particular moments of alignment
The words
"I feel you; can you feel me too?"

Teachers Salary

As a child looking up to
And at
My teachers
I was under
The impression that the more important
Your job is to society
The more you get paid
I used to think being a teacher
Was one of the safest career choices
You could make

But I heard this one tale of a New York
Teacher who quit his job to become a
Dog walker   It saved him from getting
Evicted

And another of a teacher
From Washington who quit
To become a stripper
And gave a lap dance to
A student she used to tutor after hours

So either OUR priorities are misplaced
Or MY priorities are misplaced

Lust & Envy

Go hand-in-hand
All I do is desire
Intimacy and consistency
But when I get it
It feels so fickle
That I can't feel it at all

You can like love
And use love to make you more likeable
But if it's only a tool to you
You'll find that the everlasting
Chase
Only wastes your stamina

I know this from experience
It feels like just last year
I had my first kiss
On that park bench
With a girl I'd never see again
Exposing me to bliss
My pituitary gland kicked in
Gear   I   Became a man when
She christened my lips
I've been chasing that high
Ever since

Tarot Readers

The incense queens in all these
Paisley garbs
Slurping nectar from the source

Delicate yet assertive
Like a weighted blanket

Hospitable
They caress me
And tell me the cards have my future set
I don't believe them
But they comfort me so much
And they manifest more than I do
I don't bother to refute this claim
I just nod and breathe into their
Non-religious prayers
And they make me feel so safe
I'm unsure if I believe them after all
Or if they are impeccable swindlers

Small Victory

They told me
That deli ham causes cancer
(Although what doesn't?)
I stare at in in my fridge and decide
Whether or not I want to each lunch
Tomorrow,
I figure it's worth it
And pile it on the bread
More more and
Also more   It feels like ambition
                        It feels like defiance
                        It feels like victory
But

Probably not;
What has to happen
To a person of ambition
To accept that things are
Just the way they are?

The Pros Of Complaining

If heaven is a personalized paradise
Can I travel to yours as well?
Or do I have to manifest my own version of you
From what I can recollect?

Acting like a petulant child to God
At the gates of heaven
Because it's not
What I want

I don't care who I complain to
I'll whine longwindedly
Until they let me see you again
The real you
Not the stainless masterpiece
I consider you to be
But the flawed work in progress
That always prevails

I miss that version of you

Learning Your Next Life

It's a new year
But only where
I'm at
The story of my life is best viewed in
IMAX
Yet another poem to fly overheads
Like the cuckoo's nest

The barrel's Hitch-cocked
Filming a deleted scene
The director gets his shot
Now I'm a starlet on the silver screen

Sniped with a silver bullet
On my chest a scarlet letter
It's still a new year
Father time still says it gets better

I cast a new version of me
Tenured and strict
I hope he can make out the letters
Through the blood splatter
Coated on the script

And learn from past mistakes
Ace a few more takes
A new year has dawned
We have a lot to catch up on

Screen Door

The thoughts creep in
During the slippery stretch of silence
Like leaving the screen door open
For a second too long
And a bug flies in

The worry that I'm
Prioritizing the wrong parts
Of my dreams
Focusing on the extraneous bonuses
That perceivably come along with it.
THAT one was loitering around the porch
Like a Mormon...

But me being the gullible curious
Dope I am took a chance
Now the bug comes in and all I hear
Is the vexing buzz from this
Intimidating thought

On the other hand... the bugs in MY home
Now.   Trapped in a liminal confined box
It can't get away
I let the bug stick to every wall
I mull over this thought from every angle
Investigating where the bug flew to next
Where the impetus of this issue began
And just when the hush gets too
Suspicious for both of us...
WHAP

And I'm awarded with the other shade of
Silence. That earned break from the

Drama.   I keep my screen door closed
And remember that happiness can be
Riveting without chaos.

Au Naturel

A coffee scented candle
Behind
My empty coffee mug from earlier
I neglect to wash the mug

A musky amber cologne
Versus
My deodorant and pheromones
I hope I reek delightfully

Tomato sauce cans in domino formation
Across
A packet of seeds three aisles down
I'll grow my own store

A supermodel caked in makeup
Beside
The girl plotted with pimple patches
I'm sure she's more agreeable

North Star

Life going down south
And the only light gets snuffed out
No harm
No foul
People will make a fleck of debris their
North Star
And follow it with the gruff grunting
Of a lone gunslinger
Which is the role they play
When they can't admit to themselves
That they are just socially inept

There's no idealized path
No designated structure
No North Star
It's where you will go
And where you will not return

Losers Dealing With It

Tanya was ugly
Horribly ugly
Like, yucky ugly
She tried her best at her job
She tried and failed at her job
Her ingrown hairs form
A perfect bow
Which makes her think her
Presence is a present
She has no friends

Tristan was a dunce
Dumb enough to tease him
Upfront to his face
And he wouldn't know you
Were talking about him
He tried and failed at everything
He was too dumb to keep a hobby
He felt transparent to the world
Because his efforts never transpired

There's people like this all over the place
Losers who just kinda deal with it
No one likes to talk about them
And acknowledging them sounds mean
But I think it's worth noting that some
People have it all   And   Some people
Just have to deal with it

Snakes In The Grass

I'm often leery
Well aware of any snakes
I see peeking
Through blades of grass
Sharp and fitted to their
Wiggly line of a body
Now I don't condone poaching
But I could use a new coat
And snakeskin is pricy
I'll never kill enough to make them go
Extinct
Everybody needs haters the snakes
Make you think
Make you move
Make you work
Make you look important

Snakes in the grass keep me
On point
Snakes in the grass keep me
Glued to my itinerary
Snakes in the grass keep me
Going
Snakeskin coats keep me
Fresh and warm

Broke Boy (Comfort Zone)

Not enough money for good protein
So he drizzles buffalo sauce over
                    Baked pigeon wings

                He half-asses everything
                Robs a corner store for Bic's
                            And slims
                Flees on foot
                            In shoes
                A half-size too big

He snatches pastor garments and
Uses them to kindle flames
And burn the bushes

                He can't afford to have fun
Or exercise   His contemporary's call
                Him Broke Boy
Due to his bank account and spirit
He's shunned from the comfort zone
He's too broke   He no longer cares
And as we all know:

                The comfort zone is there
                For folks who aren't good
                At not caring

Everything But My Dignity

Planned for 5:30
I knock at 6:45
The foods cold
She got impatient   Now she's full
Furrowed brow   Expensive pout
Throwing all your things out
Her anger fumes around
Into a blubbery cloud
My fine china
Plates
Raked from the cupboards
Everything is taken from me
But the kitchen sink
And inside it:
My dignity
I offered her a trade
But it gave her the upper hand
I asked for a plea deal
She saw through that act like a mime
Wrapped up her grand stand
And it left me in a bind
Because I'm still tied to my
Dignity in the kitchen sink inside

Same Boat

I ran into an old playmate
We used to rule over recess
He's got big burly pecs (man-tits, really)
We commiserate about our lives
To see who gets the bragging rights

He asks what was my major
I pull out a piece of paper
A loose leaf sheet
With a poem from last week
He looks back up like
"You trying to be funny?"
I reply
"Don't we get paid the same salary?"
I've seen
                    Tables flip
                        Salads tossed
But I didn't believe in mutiny
        Until I saw it right in front of me
He starts acting like a parody

Rocking the boat
        To prove we aren't the same
I'm thrown overboard
From his lack of tame
But I'm a born sinner and a born swimmer
I survive in droughts and I don't drown
In the waves I swear I spot a fin
                But it was just him
Reeling from the outburst I hooked
In him

We WERE in the same boat

But now it's international waters
No rules   No rights
Bragging isn't worth a life
And neither is bitching
About not being
Where you want to be in life

Worth It

Congested but you're stressed
Enough to take another hit
Next morning your lungs are
Pre-heated
Overtime the cilia
Pushes all the gunk out
Tar seeping from the chest
You're the next oil spill
Fatter than the Gulf of Mexico
A sound mind
Combined with
A sick body
Is worth it
When you hate the parts
Of your
Psyche that you can't
Survive without

Redundant

Some say
People never change
Some say
Changing is all people do
I say
Both are so true its trite
If changing is your natural state
Then changing will become repetitive
What is expected of you
And the fact that you keep changing
Will become the thing about you
That never changes

5 W's

I'm stoked to miss
Who   And   What
                  I have
When I get something
          Different
Wherever that might
Be
  But why does that
  Matter right now?

My Hands To I

I've no more prayers
I've stamped my hands to my sides
I've outstretched them for so long
Damn near demanding for help
But like everyone my arms get tired

My hands
Ready to comfort
I
The only one
Who sees my hands
I
The one who is always with me
I

Stroke Of A Lifetime

Green smells like dirty crops
Red smells like fresh apples
Blue smells like an urgent care
Yellow smells like the Grand Canyon
Orange smells like orange (naturally)
Pink smells like frosting
Purple smells like an empty frosting can
Black smells like life
White smells like death
Grey smells like the 1940's
Brown smells like burnt toast

And so do strokes

The Other Planets Don't Rock With Us

Once a year
The council of every planet in
The Solar System   (Except for Earth)
Meet up and review the behavior of
Earth
How its inhabitants have treated
Each other
And

It.

Once a year
Earth receives a failing grade
And the councils of the other planets
Decide Earth is not ready to join
The coalition
And they keep their existence
A secret from Earth
And spend another year reviewing
The covert and derivative
Ways we choose to stab each other
In the back
Creating one big gash
Out of many small gashes

You Must Be The One

Who else knows what it's like
To be you?
Trotting damp moldy roads
Supple as tissue paper

Who has done all that you've done?
Precariously balancing dozens of plates
On dozens of poles
Always ready to feed the hungry around you

Who else could be the one?
The one capable of raising hell with a pinky
And lowering it with a nod

You must be the one
The only one who can make it through
What you've been through

You must be the one
You have to be the one
You are the one

Bring Protection With You

People get killed for walking now
I'm not sure an umbrella matters anymore
When it rains
And the testimony you bowed to
During mass yesterday doesn't have
Any practical use
It was just to keep the pagans
At bay
So no one dies while walking
In the rain

Backsliding

Your face is a symbol of love to me
And your body represents debauchery
Your aroma lingers like onions and garlic
On the stove
Or used tampons in the wastebasket
It brings the room together
On second thought I might want you
To come back home
I didn't mean it
And I know you didn't either
Come back home
The mind games are worth the company
And the cold shoulder is just a misnomer
I know you didn't mean it
I didn't either
Come back home

Narc

As I slowly and sometimes
Flatteringly dip my toes into adulthood
I'm fascinated no one

Talks about how the average person
Commits like 5 crimes a day

I've known people who drive
Under the
Influence more than sober
(They're only ever California sober)

I've come to know that everyone litters
Which is easy to forget is a crime
Because everyone does it so often

People jaywalk more often than
They use crosswalks
Because a quick risk is faster
Than the flashing yield signs over yonder

And every single day someone is
Assaulted. Minor or major
Someone somewhere is always getting
Hurt and someone somewhere is always
Getting away with it

And as I dip my heels into adulthood I find
That this is just the way the world works

Evolution

I am a giant to all other species
My finger is the sun to an ant
I can
Eradicate each of them with ease
I could steal fish from the sea
Without even trying
I'm a zoned-out deity

I walk through tornadoes
And stand facing the cyclone
So the gust slicks my hair back and
Blow-dries it for me
Yet I jump at squirrels abruptly
Rustling in and out of bushes
I could crush and muddle its acorns
Under my shoe right in front of it

Evolution is a funny thing
Humans are almighty to all around us
And always exposed to ourselves

Street Performer

Cutting through Times Square
Looking for the 6 train
I passed by an all-silver street
Performer posing on top of his
Pedestal
Stiff as the Empire State Building
I walked past him
And he took his hat off
Grabbed his guitar case full of change
And walked with me

I thought he was working extra hard
For a tip from me
But he really just ended his shift
We hopped the turnstile with the
                    Same athleticism
We took the same train
We got off at the same stop
And I still couldn't tell if it was an act

We rounded the same corners
Passed the same barbershops
And only at an undeniable fork
In the road did we split
As I point myself left I look back at him
Silver and frozen once   Again
He has restarted his act
I thought "Fuck it, he's earned it"
I went to drop some quarters colored
The same as him in his guitar case
But he grabbed my fist before it opened
And like an animatronic he staggeringly
Mouthed

"Keep it. You put on a good show too"

I've Been Dreaming Recently

Let me press you
On what it takes for
Dreams to come true?
Is it earned through overcoming
Feuds with a few scrapes?
Or is it randomized for the
Right time at the right place?

I dreamt I gave myself the pride
Others dish out to me with ease
And I learned my obnoxious goals
Are unnecessarily lofty
But greatness is exaggerated effort
Plus a dreamers demeanor
I don't know what it takes
For dreams to come true
But as long as I have them
They are true to me

Quintessential Romance Poem

I thumb your rose
And you sing
That's why petals
Get plucked
I get
Pricked by the thorns
Of your stem rough
Stubs uncut
The sheer silkiness
Of your bud sends
Me swooning so
Why would
I go
Smell the roses
When I have you
Planted in this
Abode?

To Each Their Own

I see people with all the things   I
Assume I want
And I get bitter and jealous   When
They don't appreciate it   But
Those people are
Bitter and jealous as well   So
Maybe there's nothing
To appreciate in the   First
Place

We all have our own voids   To
Fill just don't make it seem like   The
Way you fill it is worth   Bragging
About

Your righteous freedom isn't   Righteous
To everyone else   It
Just looks like innocuous   Bullshit
To most of us

Astronauts Don't Go To Heaven

And to the astronauts that die in space
That is your heaven. Your cloudless
Heaven.

Die over the clouds
And you're not allowed to join them
Low oxygen makes space and
Your forlorn body an amalgamation

The astronauts that die in space missed
Paradise they're stuck in the boundless
Continuum

Shoulda stayed in bounds
Now your stoned asteroid body
Knows no bounds

Goodbye forever. I see you from my
Airy hammock
Dreaming of forever, and I ask if I can get
Your designated spot to
Extend my mansion

Nirvana Or Balance

Decree that the Buddha
Knows not what he sees
Crossed legs Closed eyes
Teaching nirvana
To the panic stricken
Too scared to leave the monastery
Closed legs Crossed eyes
An illustrious ultimatum

You Can Do It

Nerds can be drug dealers
Jocks can be terrorists
Prom queens can be arsonists

Kidnappers could be firefighters
Murderers could be detectives
Scammers could be salesmen

Value Within Each Other

I'm sorry you mean so much to me
I'm sorry I mean so much to you
One of us drops a throwaway comment
Like a piece of pocket lint
The other catches and handles it
Like a gold bar
Our love is overpriced for us
And a stereotype for
Everyone else
But fuck everyone else
This is about me and you
And the tightrope I walked
Just to get a good look at you
You kept me balanced by merely
Watching
It's no wonder
I fell off when you couldn't stand the
Sight of me wobbling like a moron

Where The Mechanical Bulls Graze

The mechanical bulls yearn for the
Opulent shamrock pastures
Thirsting for the
Ocean waters
Filtered by the coral branches

But They Were Not Made For This

They are merely tools for the
Interning cowgirls and cowboys
Who hop on the mechanical bulls
And imagine going to the same places

But They Were Not Made For This

Neither of them were given
The aptitude to ride off
Into the dawn
They just rock on top of each other
Role-playing free-range in the
Dainty   Dusk

Gorgeous Nonsense

The land of milk and honey
In my tea
Spoiled on the counter.
And as if it couldn't get any worse
My rattail is back.
I try hard to not care at all
But let me know if that's bad.
I hammered this poem on an anvil
So it won't break anymore.
This doesn't have to mean anything
If you have met me before.

Sounds like Gorgeous Nonsense
Take your time.

All these words to choose from
But do you know what they mean?
I just took the brunt of it
So, va fa Napoli.
All that pretty privilege
But you don't know what to do.
And I could see why you'd be mad
If I was you too.
I'm just trying the best I can
And I learned some things from you.

Sounds like Gorgeous Nonsense
Take your time.